The SCRIBBLE MONSTERS!™
Printing

Meet the five Scribble Monsters:
Inky, Blot, Nibs, H.B., Pablo and their pet Smudge.

Can you help me print this shape?

Blot

Smudge

Nibs

Inky

H.B.

Pablo

You will need paints, paintbrushes and various household items to finish the pictures in this book.

Rainy day

Inky and H.B. like jumping in puddles. Can you help to print more rain for them?

Mix white and a little bit of black paint to make grey.

Splish splash!

Please print lots of rain to make the puddles bigger.

Mix grey paint on a flat plate. Place a pencil onto the paint. Lift it and press it onto the page to add more rain.

Fingerprint leaves

Paint your fingertip green to print lots of leaves on the big tree.

How many birds can you see?

Fingerprint flowers

Now use your fingertip to print some pretty flowers.

buzz buzz!

How many bees can you see?

Print two flowers pink and two flowers blue.

Snowy day!

Inky and Nibs love snowy days.
Can you fill the sky with lots
of snowflakes for them?

Dip the blunt end
of a pencil into white
paint to print lots
more snowflakes.

I have made a
snowman. Can you
help Nibs make one
just like mine?

Ask a grown-up to cut a potato in half.

Paint the cut side of one half white. Press it onto the bottom circle to print my body.

Paint the potato white again. Press it onto the top circle to print the snowman's head.

Use felt-tip pens to draw in the snowman's eyes, nose and mouth. Draw in his arms and hands.

In the fish tank

Blot and Pablo are looking at the big yellow fish in the fish tank. Can you help them print more scales on its body?

Ask a grown-up to help. Cut a small potato into four, to make scale-shaped printing blocks.

Paint your printing block orange. Place onto a scale shape. Press down and lift off.

Play block town

Inky, H.B. and Pablo are using
their play blocks to print a town.

Paint one side of a play
block and quickly press
it onto the page to print
the shape.

Print your own town here.

Use different colours of paint for each shape. Don't forget to wash all the blocks off!

Fluffy clouds

Pablo and Inky love flying their planes. Can you make lots of fluffy white clouds in the sky for them?

Dip a small piece of sponge in white paint. Keep dabbing it over a cloud shape until you have made a fluffy, white cloud.

How many birds can you see?

Dip the sponge in the paint again and make another cloud shape.

Add lots of fluffy white clouds for the Scribble Monsters to hide behind.

Fun with leaves

Collect some leaves so you can make prints like Nibs, H.B. and Blot.

Use a thick paintbrush to paint one side of the leaf.

Turn the leaf over, place it onto paper and press down.

Lift off the leaf to reveal a lovely leaf print!

Use different leaf shapes and colours to fill this page with beautiful prints.

Apple print bugs

Inky and Pablo like to eat apples. Can you help them use an apple to print some bugs?

Ask a grown-up to cut an apple in half.

Paint the cut side red. Put it face down on the circle and press to print my body.

Now print six black dots using your fingerprint.

Fairytale castle

Blot is building a castle. Help Blot to print lots more orange bricks. Mix orange by adding a tiny bit of red to yellow paint.

Ask a grown-up to cut a small rectangle of sponge. Dip it in orange paint and press it onto the page to add more bricks.

You will need lots of orange paint to build a castle.

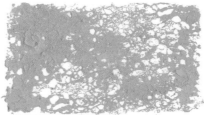

Handprint fun!

Have fun making handprints with Nibs.

I'm a scary dinosaur. Turn your book to make an upside down handprint for me!

Paint your hand blue to make your handprint dinosaur!

Use your fingertip to print red spots on me.

Blowing bubbles

Pablo loves blowing bubbles. Help Nibs and Inky to print lots of bubble shapes.

Dip the rim of a paper cup in wet paint and press it on the page to print a bubble shape.

Now use the base of the cup to make smaller circles. Find other circle shapes to print more.

Use lots of different-sized circles and colours to fill this page with beautiful bubble prints.

Jungle adventure

Nibs and H.B. are on safari and see a tiger that needs your help.

Ask a grown-up
to cut a carrot into
different stick shapes.

Place a long carrot stick in
black paint and press it onto
one of my stripes to make
it black. Please make all my
stripes black.

Blot's furry bear

Blot has printed a picture of Fluffy — his teddy bear.

I glued on two paper circles for Fluffy's eyes and bits of black paper for his nose and mouth. I used a felt-tip pen to add dots for his eyes.

Print another bear just like Fluffy. Mix
yellow, red and blue paint to make brown.
Dip the back of a plastic fork in the paint
to print furry lines for its face.

Don't forget... I need
two eyes, a black nose
and a mouth!

Pretty butterflies

The Scribble Monsters are using kitchen sponges to print some pretty butterflies.

Ask a grown-up to help you put an elastic band around the middle of a rectangular sponge.

Squirt different coloured paints from their bottles onto one half of the sponge.

Fold the sponge in two and press both halves together. Now unfold.

Print the painted sides onto the page to print a butterfly. Lift off.

Use a thin brush to paint in the butterfly's head and body.

Make your own butterfly prints here.

Leaf shapes

Nibs, Blot and H.B. have collected more leaves to show you how to make some different leaf prints.

Place a leaf on the page. Dip a sponge in paint to dab colour over the leaf.

You need to hold the leaf in place with your other hand.

Now lift off the leaf. See its shape!

Help the Scribble Monsters to fill this page with leaf prints. Use different shaped leaves and colours.

Funny faces!

I appear 15 times in this book!

Ask a grown-up to cut a potato in half, then make some potato print faces.

Use felt-tip pens to draw in their funny faces!